THE STORY
of the chicken
WITH ITS WINGS

Once upon a time the chickens didn't have wings.

They had a meeting and made a decision to ask the King of the Birds to give them wings to fly.

One of them then asked for an appointment with the king of birds

The moment came:
Chicken: Hello Mr. King
of Birds

The eagle, the king of the birds: Hello, Mr. Chicken, what do you want?

Chicken: we the chickens ask you Sir if possible to give us wings so that we can also fly like all the birds.

The eagle: I would like to give you some garlics but first you have to do me a favor.

Chicken: With pleasure Mr. King

Chicken: what can we do for you?

Eagle: You will all watch over our bean fields tomorrow. And if the bean field is intact I will give you garlic worthy of you.

Chicken: at your orders, Mr. King

The next day, all the chickens went to the bean field.

After a few hours, some chickens started to nibble on the bean leaves.

And attract the attention of the other chickens to eat too

By 3pm, the king of the birds has come to the field .

The king of the birds finds that almost all the bean leaves have been ravaged by the chickens.

The eagle: you all ate our bean leaves. I will not give you garlic!

Chicken: Please sir, you have offered us a challenge that you already know we will not keep.

Please don't do this.

Eagle: Okay, I'll give you some garlics but garlics to keep you steady.

The wings I will give you will not allow you to fly since you had no patience.

And that's how the chickens got their wings that they can't fly.